Writers and Their Work: No. 82

NORMAN DOUGLAS

202534

by

IAN GREENLEES

PUBLISHED FOR
THE BRITISH COUNCIL
and the NATIONAL BOOK LEAGUE
by LONGMANS, GREEN & CO.

Three shillings and sixpence net

Norman Douglas (1868–1952), despite a comparatively slender output, was one of the most distinguished modern writers. *South Wind*, his most successful book, has lasting qualities; and *Old Calabria* remains one of the really enthralling travel books of the present century. Although Douglas's first book did not appear until after he was forty, he lived long, seldom wrote below his best, and when he died he was recognized generally as the master of a rich and individual style.

Mr. Greenlees knew Norman Douglas well and travelled with him in many parts of Italy, a country of which Douglas was fond, and which he came to know better than many Italians. 'Douglas', says Mr. Greenlees, 'succeeded in remaining a humanist in an age which grew increasingly hostile to humanism.' His analysis and summary of Douglas's work will attract many readers, not least among his own countrymen, who relish self-criticism. Such attacks as he makes in his books on national assumptions and prejudices will induce many to re-examine them, and perhaps get them into better focus. For the British have always had a weak spot for the writer who turns their ideas upside down.

Bibliographical Series
of Supplements to 'British Book News'
on Writers and Their Work

*

GENERAL EDITOR
Bonamy Dobrée

¶ GEORGE NORMAN DOUGLAS (his names in full) was born on 8 December 1868 at Falkenhorst, Thuringen, in Austria. He died at Capri on 9 February 1952.

Islay Lyons

NORMAN DOUGLAS

NORMAN DOUGLAS

by IAN GREENLEES

PUBLISHED FOR
THE BRITISH COUNCIL
and the NATIONAL BOOK LEAGUE
BY LONGMANS, GREEN & CO., LONDON, NEW YORK, TORONTO

LONGMANS, GREEN & CO. LTD.
6 & 7 Clifford Street, London W.1
Boston House, Strand Street, Cape Town
531 Little Collins Street, Melbourne

LONGMANS, GREEN & CO. INC.
55 Fifth Avenue, New York 3

LONGMANS, GREEN & CO.
20 Cranfield Road, Toronto 16

ORIENT LONGMANS PRIVATE LTD.
Calcutta Bombay Madras
Delhi Vijayawada Dacca

First published in 1957

Printed in Great Britain at The Curwen Press, Plaistow, E.13

NORMAN DOUGLAS

NORMAN DOUGLAS was a humanist. He was many other things besides; novelist, travel-writer, essayist, geologist, botanist, biologist. He was animated by an insatiable curiosity, which extended to a great variety of subjects and countries. In a significant passage of *Alone*, when writing of children, he throws an interesting sidelight on his own point of view: 'A man who has tried to remain a mere citizen of the world and refused to squeeze himself into the narrow methods and aspirations of any epoch or country will discover that children correspond unconsciously to his multifarious interests. They are not standardized. They are more generous in their appreciations, more sensitive to pure ideas, more impersonal. Their curiosity is disinterested. The stock may be rudimentary, but the outlook is spacious; it is the passionless outlook of the sage. A child is ready to embrace the universe. And, unlike adults, he is never afraid to face his own limitations. How refreshing to converse with folks who have no bile to vent, no axe to grind, no prejudices to air; who are pagans to the core; who, uninitiated into the false value of externals, never fail to size you up from a more spiritual point of view than do their elders; who are not oozing politics and sensuality, nor afflicted with some stupid ailment or other which prevents them doing this and that.' Like the child he adumbrates here, 'he was ready to embrace the universe'.

Douglas began to write late in life. *Siren Land* was not published until 1911, when he was already forty-three. This was his first serious book, though he had published *Unprofessional Tales*, a volume of short stories, under the pseudonym of 'Normyx' in 1901, in collaboration with his wife.

He was born in 1868 at Falkenhorst, Thuringen, in Austria. His father was Scottish and his mother half Scottish and half German. He spent his early years in Austria but was educated in England, first at a preparatory school and then at Uppingham. He has written of his intense dislike of Uppingham, but after spending two years there he was able to leave and continue his education at Karlsruhe in Germany. There he was happier and was able to lay the basis of a sound scientific education. Douglas held strong views on education, and some of these are expounded by Keith in *South Wind*. 'If I had a son,' Keith says to the Bishop, 'I would take him from school at the age of fourteen, not a moment later, and put him for two years in a commercial house. Wake him up. Make an English citizen of him. Teach him how to deal with men as men, to write a straightforward business letter, manage his own money and gain some respect for those industrial movements which control the world. Next, two years in some wilder parts of the world, where his own countrymen and equals by birth are settled under primitive conditions and have formed their rough codes of society. The intercourse with such people would be a capital invested for life. The next two years should be spent in the great towns of Europe, in order to remove awkwardness of manner, prejudice of race and feeling, and to get the outward forms of a European citizen. All this would sharpen his wits, give him sure interests in life, more keys to knowledge. It would widen his horizon. Then, and not a minute sooner, to the University, where he would go, not as a child, but a man capable of enjoying its real advantages, attend lectures with profit, acquire manners instead of mannerisms and a University tone instead of a University taint.' Douglas himself did not go to a university, nor did he ever regret this. *Humani nihil a me alienum puto* would certainly have described his approach to life. He remained at the Karlsruhe Gymnasium for six years, until he reached the age of twenty.

At this period his interests lay in a scientific direction and he wrote papers in German as well as English. He was bilingual in these two languages and remained so for the rest of his life. In addition, his mastery of Italian was complete and extended to a knowledge of several Italian dialects. Even towards the end of his life he could converse at will in Russian, and his French was always fluent. He passed the Foreign Office examination in 1893 and from 1894 to 1896 was a Third Secretary at the British Embassy, St. Petersburg. He resigned from the Foreign Office in 1898, when he inherited some money. In the same year he married Elsa Fitzgibbon and they lived for the next few years in the Villa Maya, on the Bay of Posillipo, which he had bought in 1897 —later he moved to Capri, where he wrote various monographs on the island. He had first visited the island in 1888, and his love of the Mediterranean, and of Capri in particular, germinated with this first visit. He was divorced in 1903. In the years following his retirement from the Foreign Office he lived either in Capri or on the Bay of Naples, though he also travelled extensively. He was extravagant in these years and soon ran through his money, with the result that from about 1907 onwards he turned to writing to earn his living. He was fond of recounting how he had been driven to write by economic necessity, almost as if he would have preferred, given financial independence, to write scientific treatises and pursue the path of scholarship.

In the next few years he wrote *Siren Land* and *Old Calabria*, which were the result of many journeys to southern Italy. In 1909 he visited Tunisia for the second time, and in 1912 *Fountains in the Sand*, a travel book about that country, was published. From 1910 to 1916 he lived in London, and it was during part of this period that he was assistant editor of the *English Review*, under Ford Madox Ford. It was for him a period of great financial difficulty. *Old Calabria* was published in 1915 and was more successful than *Siren Land*, the first edition of which was mostly sold as waste paper. In 1916 he returned to Italy, where he earned a little money contributing impressions to the *Anglo-Italian Review*. Some of these were later collected and formed part of *Alone*. In 1916 we find him living again in Capri, at what has now become the Albergo Ercolano, and writing *South Wind*.

This was published in 1917, was the first of his books to gain a widespread success, and thus established his reputation as a writer. In 1922 Douglas settled in Florence, where he continued to live until 1937. During this period he published privately printed editions of his new works and sold them direct to the public, a system which he found financially more rewarding than publishing them through the normal channels. Later, he would sell the copyright outright to a London publisher. From 1937 to 1940 he lived in the south of France, but at the end of 1940 he moved to Lisbon and from there to London, where he arrived in January 1941. He remained for the rest of the war in England, but was always hoping to return to Italy, for which country he eventually obtained a visa in July 1946. When he first approached an Italian diplomat at the Embassy in London for a visa to return to Italy, he was told that the Italian Government were not prepared to grant visas to those who wished to live in Italy, but only to those who intended to pay a short visit to the country. To this he answered that he did not so much want to live there as to die there. This reply so moved the Italian attaché that he decided to make a special effort to get an exception made in his case and was fortunately successful in so doing.

He stopped first in Rome, where he stayed a week, and then went on to Positano, and finally back to Capri, where he remained, with the exception of an occasional visit to Rome or Calabria, until his death in 1952. Capri evoked many agreeable memories for him, and he lived in a separate apartment in the villa of his old friend, Kenneth Macpherson. He was of course aware of the great changes which had overtaken Capri, as he points out in the Postscript to the *Footnote on Capri*. 'At this moment', he wrote, 'Capri is in danger of developing into a second Hollywood and that, it seems, is precisely what it aspires to become. The island is too small to endure all these outrages without loss of dignity —the pest of so-called musicians who deafen one's ears in every restaurant, roads blocked up by lorries and cars—

steamers and motorboats disgorging a rabble of flashy trippers at every hour of the day.' But he himself had done much to make the island known. He had studied its history, fauna and flora, and he had used it as the background for *South Wind*, though, as he put it, 'the social atmosphere of Mr. Keith is distilled out of Capri—out of the Capri as it always should have been and as it never, alas, yet was or will be'.

II

Although Douglas's interests were manifold and his talents varied, it was as a writer of travel books that he excelled. He was the greatest travel writer of his generation and indeed takes his place among the great English writers of that genre. As Professor Dawkins has pointed out, he was an extrovert traveller. He was interested in the history, customs and traditions of the country or region he visited. He was amused by any eccentricities of character, and *Old Calabria* or *Siren Land*, for example, abound in conversations with individual, odd characters. An individualist himself, Douglas admired a rich, original personality in others. He despised the gradual standardization which has over-taken, and continues to overtake, contemporary society. 'Education', he wrote in *How about Europe?* 'has been raised to a bad eminence and one or two charges can be brought against it which contain more than the proverbial grain of truth. It is a centripetal process; it creates a type instead of a character; in other words, it instils uniformity, which is an enemy of civilization. None but a strong nature can profit by its good effects and defy the bad ones; none but a small percentage of children recover before middle age, when it is too late, from that withering strain of application. It frets away their finer edges and dries up the well-springs of individualism. It destroys their originality of outlook, their curiosity, their initiative, the directness of their mental vision. They learn to see with eyes, and to think with brains, which are not their own. Their impulses, their conversations—their dreams, I daresay—are standardized; and if not, a ten years' course of schooling has certainly done its best to attain that end. Education is a state-controlled machinery of echoes.'

Douglas had no use for universal education and the standardized types it produced. He had little use for any of the clichés and shibboleths so popular in his generation. He liked to think for himself. He regarded education as a voluntary process which went on throughout life, and not something which just began and ended with school. Douglas felt at home in the Mediterranean and in fact lived there the larger part of his long life, either on the Bay of Naples or in Florence. No English writer of the last fifty years has known Italy so well or interpreted it so accurately. It was a pleasure, when travelling with him, to hear him discoursing at ease with Italians in Calabria of all ages and from all walks of life. He had a predilection for the young and the very old. Already in 1934, when I first travelled with him to Calabria, he had become something of a legend there—the English writer who had published such a detailed and learned work on their region and visited it so frequently, whether climbing up Monte Pollino from Castrovillari, or walking through the Greek Sila, or the Sila Grande, carrying the familiar rucksack, and traversing great distances either on foot or on mule. The innkeeper, the chemist and schoolmaster would gather round him as he arrived unexpectedly in the primitive hostelry in some mountain village. Most of them had not even read Old Calabria for—strangely enough—it has never been translated into Italian, but they knew of it from the few who had been able to read it in English. They were flattered that he remembered and recognized them, enjoyed his laughter and his jokes and were immediately put at their ease by his courteous manner and his familiarity with their language.

His deep knowledge of the country—gained through long residence and extensive travelling—informs all his Italian travel books—*Siren Land, Old Calabria, Summer Islands* and *Alone*. But there is much more than mere knowledge of the country (this provides the background); a humanistic epicurean philosophy of life, a love of the absurd, profound scholarship, and humanity are there in abundance.

Douglas displays his learning in *Old Calabria* more than in the other travel books. It should perhaps be emphasized that his scholarship was genuine, and not, as has been suggested, just a bluff which he indulged in to mystify or impress the innocent reader. Considerable research went into the writing of *Old Calabria*; Douglas spent many weeks, first, in the National Library at Naples, and, later, in the British Museum reading and checking the sources to which he refers. He was indeed fond of relating how he acquired the habit of taking snuff while reading in the British Museum. Even Italian critics have not questioned the scholarship of *Old Calabria*.

Old Calabria is the masterpiece of Douglas. It was published in 1915, though written in the years before the war. Douglas had of course read and admired the books of many English travellers to Calabria—Keppel Craven, Swinburne, Ramage, Lear and Gissing—indeed, he writes of them himself, but his own account is more comprehensive, scholarly and ironical. Above all, as with the other travel books, it is impregnated with his personality. In *Experiments*, in the course of an essay on the *Arabia Deserta* of Doughty, he defines the qualities required by a good writer of travel books: 'it is not enough to depict, in however glowing hues, the landscape and customs of distant regions, to smother us in folklore and statistics and history and besprinkle the pages with imaginary conversations or foreign idioms by way of generating "local colour". It is not enough. We want to take our share in that interior voyage and watch how these alien sights and sounds affect the writer. If he lacks that compulsion of the spirit which is called character or lets his mind linger on contingencies hostile to frank utterance, he will be unable to supply that want and leave us dissatisfied . . .

'The modern author of travel-literature one suspects to be a greyish little person, uncommonly wide awake, perky and plausible, but somewhat deficient in personality—a kind of reporter, in fact, ready to adopt anybody's philosophy, or nobody's in particular. Those earlier ones were not of this sort. They derived, to begin with, from another stock, for voyages used to be costly undertakings. They were gentle-men scholars who saw things from their own individual angle. Their leisurely aristocratic flavour, their wholesome discussions about this and that, their waywardness and all that mercurial touch of a bygone generation—where is it now? . . .

'That mercurial touch disappears naturally when the con-ditions which gave it birth are at an end. We have ceased to be what we were, that's all. Year by year our hard-won domestic privileges have been gnawed or lopped away; the secret history of the English citizen is one long wail of liberties forfeited; we are being continentalized, standardized —a process which cannot but reflect itself in life and litera-ture. It blunts our peculiar edges. Singularity, the hall-mark of that older Anglo-Saxon, is hardly perceptible in our modern bearing or writing. We have ceased to be mad, none but a flatterer would still call us eccentric. All kinds of other factors have contributed to this result, such as improved world communications. Dr. Arnold, again, that merciless pruner of youthful individualism, has wrought a miracle of destruction so far as originality is concerned, for his energies hit hardest the very class from whom those sturdy and idiomatic, and sometimes outrageous opinions used to come.'

Douglas certainly put into practice his theories on how a travel book should be written. Contrary to what some critics have asserted, he overflowed with humanity, kindli-ness and understanding of others and these qualities make themselves felt in the pages of *Old Calabria* and his other travel books. His account of the places he visits is informative and vivacious, rouses our curiosity and makes us long to visit the country. Douglas travelled for the pleasure of learning, seeing little-known places, meeting new people— and here he always had a weakness for the simpler, more elemental type of person—and, above all, satisfying his curiosity. He succeeds in communicating this pleasure to the reader. His zest for life is sensed at once and is infectious.

Douglas wrote slowly and carefully, and *Old Calabria* is the work of several years, embodying a long and varied experience. The mood changes continually. At one moment, such as in the chapters dedicated to the Flying Monk and Southern Saintliness, Douglas reveals his interest in hagiology, and shows his delicate sense of irony. At another moment he sets out to prove—perhaps with his tongue in his cheek—that Milton had in *Paradise Lost* plagiarized the *Adamo Caduto* of Salandra. Then there are passages where Douglas expresses a mood of complete serenity, as for example:

'Meanwhile it is good to rest here, immovable but alert, in the breathless hush of noon. Showers of benevolent heat stream down upon this desolation, not the faintest wisp of vapour floats upon the horizon; not a sail, not a ripple, disquiets the waters. The silence can be felt. Slumber is brooding over the things of earth . . .

'Such torrid splendour, drenching a land of austerest simplicity, decomposes the mind into corresponding states of primal contentment and resilience. There arises before our phantasy a new perspective of human affairs; a suggestion of well-being, wherein the futile complexities and disharmonies of our age shall have no place . . . To discard these wrappings, to claim kinship with some elemental and robust archetype, lover of earth and sun . . .

'How fair they are, these moments of golden equipoise.'

Compare that with the concluding paragraph of *By the Ionian Sea*, where George Gissing, after having been shown by the curator of the Museum of Reggio Calabria a few words written in Greek in the hand of François Lenormant, writes:

'I could have desired no happier incident for the close of my journey. By lucky chance this visit to the museum had been postponed till the last morning, and, as I idled through the afternoon about the Via Plutino, my farewell mood was in full harmony with that in which I had landed from Naples upon the Calabrian shore; so hard a thing to catch and to retain, the mood corresponding perfectly to an intellectual bias—hard, at all events, for him who cannot shape his life as he will and whom circumstance ever menaces with dreary harassment. Alone and quiet, I heard the washing of the waves; I saw the evening fall on cloud-wreathed Etna, the twinkling lights come forth upon Scylla and Charybdis; and as I looked my last toward the Ionian Sea I wished it were mine to wander endlessly amid the silence of the ancient world, today and all its sounds forgotten.'

How different is the mood, and how different their approach to life! Douglas, although he admired Gissing, had the more rounded and harmonious personality; and he was also more fortunate in that he was able to spend the greater part of his life in Italy. In *Alone* he asks himself why people trouble to go to Italy and replies:

'A periodical visit to this country seems an ordinary and almost automatic proceeding—a part of one's regular routine, as natural as going to the barber or to Church. Why seek for reasons? They are so hard to find. One tracks them to their lair and lo! there is another one lurking in the background, a reason for a reason.

'The craving to be in contact with beauty and antiquity, the desire for self-expression, for physical well-being under that drenching sunshine, which, while it lasts, one curses lustily; above all, the pleasure of memory and reconstruction at a distance. For a haze of oblivion is formed by lapse of time and space; a kindly haze which obliterates the thousand fretting annoyances wherewith the traveller's path in every country is bestrewn . . . He forgets them; forgets that weltering ocean of unpleasantness and remembers only the sporadic islets—those moments of calm delight or fiercer joy which he would fain hold fast for ever. He does not come here on account of a certain fountain which ought never to be cleaned. He comes for the sake of its mirage, that sunny phantom which will rise up later out of some November fog in another land. Italy is a delightful place to remember, to think and talk about. And is it not the same with England? Let us go there as a tourist—only as a tourist. How attractive one finds its conveniences and even its conventionalities, provided one knows, for an absolute certainty, that one will never be constrained to dwell among them.

'What lovely things one could say about England, in Timbuktoo!'

Douglas's travel books are full of such golden moments of happiness induced by the atmosphere of the place he is visiting—usually rich in historical associations—or the companion with whom he is travelling. The concluding passage of *Alone* conjures up such a mood:

'I thought of certain of my fellow creatures. I often think of them. What were they now doing? Taking themselves seriously and rushing about, as usual, haggard and careworn —like those rapacious ants that scurry hither and thither and stare into each other's faces with a kind of desperate imbecility, when some sportive schoolboy has kicked their ridiculous nest into the air and upset all their solemn little calculations.

'As for ourselves, we took our ease. We ate and drank, we slumbered awhile, then joked and frolicked for five hours on end, or possibly six. I kept no count of what was said nor how the time flew by. I only know that when at last we emerged from our ambrosial shelter the muscles of my stomach had grown sore from the strain of laughter and Arcturus was twinkling overhead.'

Although Douglas knew Italy and the Italians well, he was most familiar with the area south of Rome—the Sabine hills, the Abruzzi, the Bay of Naples, and Calabria. He liked classical Italy, and was drawn to those regions where the civilizations of Greece and Rome met and mingled. He had little knowledge of Italian literature, and in fact read little Italian poetry, and few novels or short stories. Neither was he interested in Italian painting nor in any kind of painting. Although he lived many years in Florence, he was prone to dismiss the architecture and pictures there with a contemptuous tone of voice as so much 'Cinquecento'. He was fascinated by the fauna and the flora of Italy. In addition to his love of pagan Italy for its associations with the past he appreciated the day-to-day human contacts. His approach was thus utterly different from that of the aesthete or intellectual who saw in Italy one vast museum and ignored the vitality and humanity of the country and its people. Douglas, with his historical and scientific cast of mind, liked classical Italy, but he needed and sought the human companionship of ordinary simple Italians as well. He had a great feeling for landscape, but, particularly, for the wild, grandiose, mountainous country of the south.

The personality of Douglas vibrates in almost every paragraph of his works, and most emphatically in his travel books. Although *Old Calabria*, *Siren Land*, or *Fountains in the Sand* fill you with a longing to visit the places described, it is possible to derive great pleasure from reading them without having travelled in one or the other of these regions, as they are knit together by the rich personality of the author, and his philosophy of life. He had all the attributes of the perfect traveller: he liked walking immense distances and he did not mind roughing it in order to see out of the way places: he could put up with coarse food and wine for the sake of getting to know remote villages in southern Italy or Tunisia: he was a fine classical scholar and could relate the present to the past: he delighted in the casual conversation: and, above all, his richly stored mind was illumined by a restless curiosity. During his travels he found great pleasure in whiling away the evening in the company of those he met in inns or restaurants. As he wrote in *Old Calabria*:

'This meal [dinner] marks the termination of my daily tasks; nothing serious is allowed to engage my attention, once that repast is ended. I call for a chair and sit down at one of the small marble-topped tables in the open street and watch the crowd as it floats around me, smoking a Neapolitan cigar and imbibing, alternately, ices and black coffee until, towards midnight, a final bottle of *vino di Cirò* is uncorked, fit seal for the labours of the day.' He made it a rule never to work after dinner and he liked to linger long over the table, talking and drinking far into the night. Douglas was always good company, but he was at his best when travelling. I can remember many journeys with him in the thirties, through Calabria, or walks across the hills near Rome, visiting places like Olevano, Genazzano, Subiaco or Arsoli; and, although he was already well past sixty, he would think nothing of walking twenty miles a day. The hours would pass quickly as he evoked memories of previous visits or would point out some rather unusual wild flower, or would recall some strange story connected with the village we passed through.

At the end of a long day's walking—and he nearly always carried a rucksack on these journeys—in Calabria or over the hills round Rome he would make for some inn which he knew and where he was received as an old friend. He attached great importance to the inns or restaurants on his travels, and would remember very clearly those which were good. He would order his meal with meticulous care, even in a Calabrian village. He attached importance to what he ate and despised those who were indifferent to food. Of an Englishman in *Alone* who remarks that he does not care what he eats, he comments: 'I don't care what I eat! What a confession to make! Is it not the same as saying, I don't care whether I am dirty or clean? . . . It is nothing to boast of. A man owes something to those traditions of our race which has helped to raise us above the level of the brute. Good taste in viands has been painfully acquired; it is a sacred trust. Beware of gross feeders. They are a menace to their fellow creatures. Will they not act, on occasion, even as they feed? Assuredly they will. Everybody acts as he feeds.'

III

In those travels through Calabria he would often be joined after dinner by those he had known on previous visits. I remember visiting S. Demetrio Corone (which he describes in *Old Calabria*) with him in 1935. We stayed at a little inn that had a few rooms above a grocer's shop. The inn-keeper, a sturdy, thick-set Albanian, with closely shaven head, owned the shop as well as the hotel. He had known Douglas for more than twenty years and said he was the first Englishman to have visited that village—at least in his lifetime. While we were dining, the secretary of the local Fascist party came in and in rather an insolent manner asked us if we had reported to the Fascio. We had, of course, filled in the usual forms at the hotel which foreigners were supposed to complete but neither of us had ever heard that there was any law obliging foreigners to go to the headquarters of the local Fascist party. This man was evidently exceeding his authority. A crowd of villagers gathered round, wondering what Douglas was going to say. He replied very calmly that we had filled up the usual forms, but did not feel that we were obliged to do anything more. The Secretary, evidently accustomed to bullying, then adopted a yet ruder tone and peremptorily shouted at us that we should have gone round to the Fascio; at this Douglas rose to his feet and declared roundly that he had visited S. Demetrio long before the Secretary was even born, had never gone to the Fascio before and did not propose to do so now. He concluded by saying that he did not want his meal to be interrupted further by such nonsense. To the delight of those assembled the Secretary remained speechless and beat a hasty retreat from the room. We resumed our dinner, and the professor, lawyer, doctor and others who had witnessed the scene were grateful that at last someone had called the bluff of this absurdly arrogant official. They all sided with Douglas, and for the rest of the evening he was the hero of these simple villagers.

'It reveals a personality. It contains a philosophy of life', was how he summed up *The Nooks and By-ways of Italy* by Crauford Tait Ramage. And no words could more appropriately or more succinctly describe Douglas's own travel books. Whether in *Old Calabria, Siren Land, Alone* or one of the other travel books, you continually catch a glimpse of Douglas himself. *Old Calabria*, in addition, contains a mass of information about the country and its social and economic conditions; there are also many shrewd, illuminating observations about the Italian character. One young man describes how he had heard that they still hang murderers in England, as they used to do in Italy. He thought this rather barbaric. Douglas adds that the people there tend to regard the English as savages, as hopeless savages. Or again: 'I pause, to observe parenthetically that this habit of uttering platitudes in the grand manner as though disclosing an idea of vital novelty (which Charles Lamb, poor fellow, thought peculiar to natives of Scotland) is as common among Italians as among Englishmen. But vested in sonorous Latinisms, the staleness of such remarks assumes an air of profundity.' He singles out the extraordinary aptitude of Italians as engineers. He points out that no people are more fundamentally sane in matters of the heart than the southern Italians. They are seldom naïvely enamoured. They may play to the gallery and act the part for a time of passionate lovers, but in their real courtship they will be realistic and marry a girl with a dowry and will be guided by the advice of their uncles and aunts, but not until their military service is terminated. 'Everything in its proper time and place.' He asserts that envy is the most conspicuous native vice, and he blames this on the lack of nutrition, and, in particular, on that morning thimbleful of black coffee. He emphasizes the poverty of Calabria. It is not very different today, though post-war Italian governments have indeed made a serious attempt to ameliorate conditions. Sometimes, re-reading *Old Calabria*, I find it difficult to remember that it was written so many years before *Christ Stopped at Eboli* (by Carlo Levi), since it anticipates so much of what is to be found in the later book. Both give accurate pictures of two different regions of southern Italy. Take, for instance, the following passage from *Old Calabria*: 'We are disposed to associate squalor with certain artistic effects, but it may be said of this and many other Calabrian places that they have solved the problem how to be ineffably squalid without being in the least picturesque.'

He remarks that Calabria is not a land to traverse alone: 'It is too wistful and stricken, too deficient in those externals that conduce to comfort.' But then Douglas seldom travelled alone. He nearly always travelled with a friend, or, as in *Alone*, found his company along the way. His acute understanding of the Italian character is displayed in the series of shrewd observations which enrich and enliven the pages of his Italian travel books. For example, in *Siren Land*, the first of his travel books, he describes the country near Sorrento. It is less erudite than *Old Calabria* but remains one of the most delightful of his books. There is the same blending of scholarship, irony and humanity. He expresses a mood of extraordinary serenity. There is a chapter on Tiberius and one on the Blue Grotto at Capri. There is a remarkable chapter on leisure in which he writes: 'Everything which distinguishes man from animals is the result of leisure . . . Leisure first made man formidable on earth. And our virtue, so far as it differs from that of animals, is purely the result of leisure . . . Leisure is the curse of the poor in spirit.'

Douglas possessed a robust sanity of outlook which stood him in good stead and which is the most distinguishing characteristic of his writing. He believed that civilized man had the right to leisure, though he should know how to use it properly. As examples of the misuse of leisure he quotes toothache, baldness, picnics, envy, fraud, codes of honour among schoolboys, army officers, and 'other imperfectly civilized associations'. Douglas, like Gissing, did not believe that time was money, but rather that money was time.

Incidentally, when regretting in *Siren Land* the untimely

death of Gissing, he attributes this to 'inefficient equipment, not of intellectuality but of outlook and attitude . . . of that tough, cheerful egotism which, sanely regarded, is but sanity itself'. Douglas prided himself on possessing a certain dose of that cheerful egotism.

In addition to the Italian travel books (*Old Calabria, Siren Land, Alone* and *Summer Islands*) he wrote *Together* (about Austria), *Fountains in the Sand* (about Tunisia), and *One Day* (about Athens). In *Together* he describes a visit to the region of Austria where he was born. He evokes a mood of nostalgia as he recalls episodes of his childhood and portrays pictures of his different relations. He points a contrast between Austria and the south, partly by quoting the reactions of R, his French travelling companion, and partly by reminding us of the difference in temperature and atmosphere between Austria and Italy. *Together*, unlike Douglas's other travel books, is lively with appreciation of the north; the shade of the woods in summer, the fir trees and pines in the Lutz forest, the mountain streams, the generous hospitality and friendliness of the Austrians—it would almost give the impression of having been written in a mood of nostalgia, after many years of residence in the south.

One Day originated out of a suggestion made by the Greek Government that Douglas should write a book about Greece rather in the manner of *Old Calabria*; for this purpose he received a grant from the Greek Government. But, unfortunately for posterity, when Douglas arrived in Athens he stayed at the British School. There he glanced at the vast library of books about Greece and he perceived what a formidable task he had set himself. It would clearly take him several years to write such a book. Moreover he realized that his knowledge of the language had grown rusty with the passage of years. He therefore abandoned such an ambitious task and contented himself with writing an account of a day's visit to one or two favourite haunts, in or near Athens, evoking memories of previous visits and giving rein to a few historical disquisitions. The result is a little masterpiece and was later republished in the volume *Three of Them*, with *Nerinda*, and *On the Herpetology of the Grand Duchy of Baden*.

In *Fountains in the Sand* he writes of his visits to Tunisia at the beginning of the century and gives some superb descriptions of the landscape and life in the towns of Gafsa and Tozeur. The conversations with some of the local inhabitants are perhaps among the most striking memories of this book.

Douglas had a zest for travelling, and derived from it an intense pleasure which he communicates in his writing. 'There is this advantage', he writes in *Late Harvest*, 'in the writing of books when they are in some measure autobiographical, describing events from childhood onwards; instead of being confused memories they are authentic documents which allow a man to live his life over again and cast his thoughts backwards with assurance. There is nothing vague about a written record.' And this is perhaps the best commentary on his travel books.

South Wind, that strange, gay, fanciful novel, also contains much of Douglas's philosophy of life. It is as if, in the interval between writing *Old Calabria* and *South Wind*, his point of view had clarified so that he expresses it in the novel in a more sharply outlined form. Although *Old Calabria* remains —for me at any rate—his finest work, *South Wind* made a greater impact and reached a wider public. It might, I suppose, be described as a novel of conversation, or a novel of ideas, rather in the manner of the novels of Thomas Love Peacock. Yet there is, as Douglas has pointed out in *Alone*, a plot. Indeed, he asserts that 'it would be nearer the truth to say that it is nothing but plot from beginning to end. How to make murder palatable to a bishop: that is the plot. How? You must unconventionalize him and instil into his mind the seeds of doubt and revolt. You must shatter his old notions of what is right. It is the only way to achieve this result, and I would defy the critic to point to a single incident or character or conversation in the book which does not further the object in view. The good Bishop soon finds himself among new influences; his sensations, his intellect, are assailed from within and without. Figures such as those in Chapters 11, 18 and 35, the endless dialogue in the boat, the even more tedious happenings in the local law-court, the very externals—the jovial immoderation of everything and everybody: they foster a sense of violence and insecurity; they all tend to make the soil receptive to new ideas.'

Indeed, the Bishop, an Anglican Bishop, who is a typical representative of the narrow, conventional upper middle classes in England, a product of the English public schools— is profoundly influenced by his brief sojourn in the Mediterranean. It might almost be described as a study of the impact made by Italy on an Englishman: *L'inglese italianizzato è il diavolo incarnato*, runs the Italian proverb. Italy certainly has a leavening, softening and civilizing influence on the Englishman who settles in, or even visits, the country. The arteries of the Bishop, which have hardened over the years, begin to soften, his conventional point of view becomes less formal, his mind more open. His values, too, change imperceptibly. He had been taught to believe that strenuousness by itself was something to be admired. Count Caloveglia points out to him that whenever anything, however fantastic, is imposed upon men by physical forces, they straight-away make a God of it and that this is why they deify strenuousness. The complex conditions under which men live in the north make life more of a struggle. They have to obtain extra clothing, footwear, mufflers, carpets and rugs; abundant and costly food is required to keep the body healthy; they have to contend with the difficulties of plumbing, gas, the woodwork, the paintings and repaintings, the tons of fuel, the lighting in winter, the contrivances against frost and rain, the never-ending repairs to houses. Such difficulties scarcely exist in the Mediterranean. Count Caloveglia makes it clear he is not interested in the majority—he dismisses these scornfully—but in the elect few. 'Living in our lands', he says to the Bishop, 'men would have leisure to cultivate nobler aspects of their nature. They would be accessible to purer aspirations, worthier delights. They would enjoy the happiness of sages. What other happiness deserves the name? In the Mediterranean, Mr. Heard, lies the hope of humanity.' The Bishop listened and was thoughtful. He brooded about happiness. At one time he used to think it was achieved by Christianity and civilization. In China he learnt that men could be happy without Christianity, and in Africa that they could be happy without civilization. Count Caloveglia, after a pause, moves relentlessly on in pursuit of his argument. He maintains that men have realized the baseness of mercantile and military ideals and will settle round the Mediterranean, there to lead serener lives. The Bishop, 'who knew something of the evils of northern industrialism', listened approvingly.

It is interesting to trace the development of the Bishop's mental processes as the story unfolds. Keith and Count Caloveglia are the main influences on him though from afar he admires Eames too. Douglas expresses his own philosophy of life partly through Keith, partly through Caloveglia, and partly through Eames. Whether in his diatribe against poverty or his enthusiasm for Pepys or his admiration for George Gissing, Keith seems to be the mouthpiece of Douglas himself. Keith, too, undermines the solid convictions of the Bishop. In a conversation with him he talks of the *demi-vierge* concessions which the English Church has made to common sense and which afford seductive resting places to the intellectually weak-kneed. Mr. Heard was slightly perturbed by these words. A good fellow like Keith! '*Demi-vierge* concessions to common sense.' What did he mean by that? Did his church really make such concessions?

'I'll think about it tomorrow,' he decided.

Later, Keith remarks to the Bishop that his values appear to be perverted, and the latter begins to wonder whether this is really so. Then Keith engages him in conversation while visiting a grotto in a rowing boat, and draws a distinction between horizontal and vertical gods. The horizontal or downstairs gods are those which were invented by intellectualists who felt themselves capable of maintaining a kind of comradeship with their deities. The vertical gods are those invented by the proletariat for the use of the aristocracy. The proletariat loves to humiliate itself, and therefore manufactures a god who approves of grovelling, a god who can look down upon them. Such a distinction had never occurred to Mr. Heard before, with the result that he was puzzled, and still more preoccupied about his values. He consoled himself, however, by pointing out to Keith that the laws of morality have at least been written down for our guidance in letters that never change. Keith counters this by describing how the laws of good conduct do change from generation to generation, and he adds that all morality is a generalization, and all generalizations are tedious. Mr. Heard asks Keith whether he does not disapprove of Van Koppen's (an American millionaire) ladies. Keith says he cannot disapprove of things which do not impinge on his activities.

'Is that your quarrel with what you call the upstairs god system?' asks the Bishop.

'Precisely. It does not offend me by its unsanitary tendency to multiply sins. It affects me when it impinges on my own activities; that is to say, when it transforms those sins into legal crimes. How would you like to be haled before a Court of law for some ridiculous trifle, which became a crime only because it used to be a sin and became a sin only because some dyspeptic or impotent old antediluvian was envious of his neighbours' pleasure. Our statute-book reeks of discredited theories of conduct; the serpent's trail of the theologian, of the reactionary, is over all.' The Bishop's significant comment is: 'It never struck me in that light before.' Mr. Heard is influenced by what he himself terms the Pagan light of the Mediterranean; for the first time in many years he has the leisure in which to meditate and is no longer drugged by habit or a life of action. He succumbs to the fascination, first, of his conversations with Caloveglia, a wise pagan Italian, and, later, of those with Keith, a self confessed hedonist. His outlook undergoes a steady change as a consequence.

Keith gives the Bishop no relief and hammers away mercilessly at his fixed preconceptions. Mr. Heard is worn down by the combined effect of the heat and the discussion and is in no mood to argue. He has just the energy to ask him his opinion.

The novel is brought to a conclusion by a conversation between Count Caloveglia and Mr. Heard; the latter asks the Count if he has noticed that there is an unwonted sparkle in the air, something cleansing and clarifying.

'To be sure I do,' replied the other, 'And I can tell you the cause of it. Sirocco is over for the present. The wind has shifted to the north. It brightens all nature. It makes one see things in their true perspective, doesn't it?'

'That is exactly what I feel,' said Mr. Heard. And the novel ends on this note, the author having accomplished his purpose of demonstrating the influence of environment on an ordinary, conventional human being.

IV

South Wind, of course, contains a great deal besides the story of the Bishop. Count Caloveglia and Mr. Keith, the two principal characters, might, as I have already pointed out, be regarded as illustrating two facets of the author's personality. Though not in every detail—for example, Douglas had a love and understanding of music which is not shared by Keith—the author uses them to express his philosophy of life—the philosophy of a temperate Epicurean, steeped in the classical tradition, a tolerant sceptic, a rationalist humanist. Douglas wrote that *South Wind* was the result of his craving to escape from the wearisome actualities of life and that his aim had been to picture himself living in a society of such instability, such 'jovial immoderation' and 'frolicsome perversity' that even a respectable bishop could be persuaded to approve of murder.

Mr. Keith resembled Douglas in that 'he was in love with life. It dealt fairly with him. It made him loth to bid farewell to this gracious earth and the blue sky overhead, to his cooks and his books, his gardeners and roses and flaming cannas; loth to exchange these things of love, these tangible delights, for a hideous and everlasting annihilation'. Constantly Douglas himself would talk in this vein. Just as Keith loved life and hated the idea of death so Douglas, speaking of himself in *Late Harvest*, writes: 'Having reached nearly twice the age at which Platen died, I no longer complain of how I squandered my days; my one regret is that I have not many more of them to squander. If one has enjoyed life and contrived to extract matter of mirth out of its not infrequent mistakes, one cannot be said to have squandered one's days. A man's days are his own. He will do well, I should think, not to listen to others as to whether he has wasted his life or not; that is his own concern. Let him analyse the past and draw conclusions, if it amuses him, as to the part he played or was made to play.'

Even in the last twilight years, at Capri, he enjoyed life; he was a rare example of the intellectual who had discovered the secret of happiness, and he had the ability to infect others with his mood. He was essentially extrovert and inclined to pity those who were given to moods of introspection. His tireless intellectual curiosity, and his capacity for enthusiasm, no doubt contributed in part to his happiness and his joy in life. A few days before he died, when he knew there was no longer any hope of recovery he remarked to a friend how tragic it was that he should have to die while so many others who did not care about life should be able to go on living. Keith, in *South Wind*, we may remember, disliked funerals and displayed an unreasoning hatred of death, and what was still more remarkable, not the least shame in confessing it. Keith, too, like Douglas, was ever avid of fresh things and regretted his lost opportunities.

The advice Keith gave to Denis was much the same as the advice Douglas was wont to give to the young: he should not attach too much importance to what human beings said and did, he should forsake art and books for a time and come into contact with nature and think things out for himself instead of listening to other people.

Like Keith, Douglas's recipe for happiness was to find everything useful and nothing indispensable, and everything wonderful and nothing miraculous; and at the same time to reverence the body and avoid first causes like the plague.

Similarly, there was much of Douglas in Caloveglia. There was something Greek about both of them. Colour— at least in art—said little to either of them, and both were enamoured of form. Like the Count, Douglas would—and sometimes did—cook *con amore* if he had the leisure and materials. Just as when Caloveglia extols the art of cooking to the Bishop so when he contrasts progress with civilization, or compares northern ethical values with those prevalent in the Mediterranean, or talks of the withering influence of the Bible on the English spirit, we seem to hear the voice of Douglas. And, above all, when the Count defines the meaning of temperance.

'Temperance,' said the Bishop. 'Another of those words I am always being obliged to use. Pray tell us, Count, what you mean by temperance.'

'I should call it the exercise of our faculties and organs in such a manner as to combine the maximum of pleasure with the minimum of pain.'

'But who is to judge what constitutes the dividing line between use and abuse?'

'We cannot, I imagine, do better than go to our own bodies for an answer to that question. They will tell us exactly how far we may proceed with impunity.'

'In that case,' said the millionaire, 'if you drink a little too much occasionally, only occasionally I mean, you would not call that intemperance?'

'Certainly not,' said the Count.

Douglas believed in the Greek virtue of moderation. He had imbibed much of what he termed the Mediterranean spirit, and latterly he was only really happy living in the south. He was in sympathy with the temperate way of life of the Italians. He liked their tolerance, their lack of hypocrisy, their pagan outlook. He liked, too, the easy-going rhythm of life, the lack of petty restrictions, such as the licensing laws. England, on the other hand, he liked to savour in small doses, rather as a tourist. In the Mediterranean, as Caloveglia pointed out, ethical standards of criticism are replaced by artistic standards, and this appealed to Douglas.

Again, in the distinction which Caloveglia draws between progress and civilization it is, I think, possible to detect Douglas's own view. He regarded progress as a centripetal movement, obliterating man in the mass, while civilization he considered a centrifugal force, permitting and postulating the assertion of personality. In his view progress subordinates, while civilization co-ordinates. The individual emerges in civilization, but is submerged in progress. The two are incompatible.

Douglas was an individualist. He was not interested in politics and believed it was the duty of the individual to carve out his own existence. He abhorred any form of intolerance. He agreed with his friend Oscar Levy that the origins of both Hitlerism and Bolshevism could be traced to the Bible. Referring to *The Idiocy of Idealism* of Levy, he wrote: 'The first (Hitlerism) he argues, has its roots in the Chosen People and pure-Race nonsense with which the Old Testament is saturated (good specimens in Ezra and Nehemiah) and which was eagerly sucked in by those passionate Bible-readers, the Germans, who twisted it into their contemptible Herrenvolk doctrine. The second has its roots in that envy of the rich which crops up repeatedly in the New Testament (Woe unto you that are rich, etc.; it is easier for a camel, etc.; conveniently contrary texts, as usual, are at hand). Would it be right to say that Christianity is based to an overwhelming extent on envy of the rich and glorification of the proletariat, that Bolshevism is based on Christianity, even as Hitlerism is based on the Hebrew prophets?'

Thus *South Wind*, behind its gay façade, has an underlying serious purpose—the projection of Douglas's Epicurean philosophy of life. But there are other characters to whom, perhaps, a brief reference should be made. Miss Wilberforce (note the irony in the choice of the name), the incurable but happily drunken spinster; Denis, the eternal adolescent, groping his way towards a knowledge of himself; Mr. Parker, the slightly shady, coarse-grained secretary of the local club; Signor Malipizzo, the opportunist, free-thinking judge; and, of course, the Russian characters.

Writing about *South Wind* in *Late Harvest*, Douglas declared that, in austere moments, certain passages struck him as being ornate to the verge of flabbiness. It is true that his style underwent a considerable change in his later books. It became more astringent, and in *Alone* he evolved a highly individual style which at times was almost conversational.

The other two novels, *They Went* (1920) and *In the Beginning* (1927) were less successful. Douglas described *They Went* as a 'little allegory of beauty versus betterment'. Just as in *South Wind* the author is concerned with morals, in *They Went* he deals with beauty and *In the Beginning* with religion. They are both presented as myths. As Professor Dawkins puts it:

'We find ourselves in fact facing that well-known Triad, the True, the Beautiful and the Good. Here we are accustomed to seeing the orthodox philosopher performing a few manipulations very much as a conjuror handles his rabbits. He rolls them about a little, lowers the light a moment and then shows us with triumph that the three white rabbits are really only three aspects of one white rabbit and that none of the children need be frightened . . . He just leaves the three poles apart to fight out their triangular duel, and so far from being all of them comfortably co-equal, the True, and very certainly the Good, tend to become rather hazy in their outlines, and the Beautiful proves herself a most aggressive and incompatible bedfellow. *South Wind* came first: in it the Good distinctly goes to the wall. Then came *They Went*; here the Beautiful seems simply indifferent to what happens to the others. Lastly we have *In the Beginning*, where we see that the sanity of Truth seems to have deserted mankind for good and all. But what has driven her away? Alas! It is Goodness, that fell disease.'

Douglas succeeded in remaining a humanist in an age which grew increasingly hostile to humanism. He carved out his own existence. He had a refreshing way of thinking for himself, and was not deceived or misled by the platitudes or shibboleths of the world around him. He knew what he wanted in life, and he made every effort to obtain it. He was happy and able to communicate his happiness and enthusiasm to others.

As he wrote in *Together*, he would not have missed the enjoyment of this life for anything, nor would he have exchanged it even then for any other creature on earth. He was at his ease with people of all kinds. If he were set down in farthest Cathay, he wrote in *Alone*, he would undertake to find, soon afterwards, some person with whom he was quite prepared to spend the remaining years of his life. In *Alone*, too, he wrote:

'I never pass that way now without thanking God for a misspent youth. Why not make a fool of yourself? It is good fun while it lasts; it yields mellow mirth for later years, and are not our fellow-creatures, those solemn buffoons, ten times more ridiculous? Where is the use of experience if it does not make you laugh?'

This Epicurean philosophy of life, adapted to the needs of the modern age, he expressed directly or indirectly in all his books. In an easy, lucid, polished prose he expressed ideas which ran counter to many of the more fashionable, ill-digested views of his day. He always seemed, however, to be talking the language of common sense. He railed against hypocrisy, puritanism and smugness. He was the least pompous and most human of men, and the least complacent and most erudite of writers; and much knowledge of life, as well as considerable pleasure, can still be derived from reading his various books.

§

Douglas is a curiously isolated phenomenon in the literary history of the last fifty years. It is difficult to place him in relation to other writers. He does not fit into any school or category. He had few points of resemblance with his own, and fewer still with the present generation. But he would have preferred it so. His writings have that timeless quality which prevents them from being dated. *South Wind* or *Old Calabria* are as fresh today as when they were first written. He did not want to conform to any pattern. He was an individualist who did not feel bound by the conventions of society or of his age. He wrote naturally and superbly but he never aspired to move in any kind of literary circle. He kept himself aloof from cliques, and his conversation concentrated on life rather than on literature . . . The cast of his mind was scientific, and he was primarily interested in facts and ideas. *South Wind* is a novel of ideas; he chooses the medium of the novel simply to expound his ideas, his philosophy of life, which he had already expressed to a great extent in *Old Calabria*. In *South Wind* he puts forward his ideas in a more playful, fanciful manner. Some of his characters hardly come to life; Denis, for example, remains hazy and formless. Some might say that the Bishop undergoes his intellectual and moral evolution too rapidly. It might strike the reader as improbable that such a transformation could take place in only twelve days.

Perhaps, too, the Bishop does not offer enough resistance to the influences surrounding him. Yet *South Wind* is not a novel in the traditional sense of the word and Douglas's purpose was to propound certain ideas while at the same time amusing the reader. And in this he was most successful.

The novelist's touch is lacking in *They Went* and *In the Beginning*; in each he is mainly concerned with advancing a thesis. He was at his happiest and most successful in the travel books; there he was able to expound his philosophy of life, express the many facets of his glittering personality, and indulge in his quest for knowledge; he was further able to record his impressions of the landscape and people he encountered in the course of his travels. Yet the same, dominant personality pervades *South Wind*, as it does the travel books, *Looking Back* or *London Street Games*, and his message in the world of today is perhaps even more relevant than it was twenty-five years ago. Just as Douglas was a sun worshipper, so the lesson he has to teach us is radiant with the sunlit atmosphere of the pagan south, and is impregnated with the robust sanity of his outlook.

NORMAN DOUGLAS

A Select Bibliography

(Place of publication London, unless stated otherwise)

Bibliographies:

A BIBLIOGRAPHY, by E. D. MacDonald. With Notes by Norman Douglas. Philadelphia (1927).

LATE HARVEST, by Norman Douglas (1946). Includes Douglas's own notes on some of his publications.

CATALOGUE OF MEMORIAL EXHIBITION, by C. Woolf and A. Anderson (1952). Held at Edinburgh Central Library.

A BIBLIOGRAPHY, by C. Woolf (1954).

Selections:

AN ALMANAC (1945). Made by the author from his own works.

NORMAN DOUGLAS: A SELECTION (1955). With a valuable Introduction by D. M. Low.

Separate Works:

ZUR FAUNA SANTORINS, Leipzig (1892). *Essay.* Reprinted from *Zoologischer Anzeiger.*

CONTRIBUTIONS TO AN AVIFAUNA OF BADEN (1894). *Essay.* Reprinted from *The Zoologist.*

ON THE HERPETOLOGY OF THE GRAND DUCHY OF BADEN (1894). *Essay.* Reprinted from *The Zoologist,* 1891, with corrections. Included in *Three of Them,* 1930.

REPORT ON THE PUMICE STONE INDUSTRY OF THE LIPARI ISLANDS (1895). *White Paper.*

ON THE DARWINIAN HYPOTHESIS OF SEXUAL SELECTION (1895). *Essay.* Reprinted from *Natural Science.* Reprinted in *English Miscellany,* Rome, 1951.

UNPROFESSIONAL TALES BY 'NORMYX' (Norman Douglas) (1901).
Fiction. In collaboration with his wife, Elsa Fitzgibbon.
Includes: 'A Mystery', 'Elfwater', 'The Sentence', 'Nerinda',
'Impromptu', 'Nocturne', 'In the Red Sea', 'Anacreontic', 'The
Ignoble', 'A Tyrrhenian Fable', 'The Case of Mrs. Hillier', 'To
E.F.G.', 'The Devil's Oak', 'The Psychological Moment', 'The
Meeting of Autos and Eschata', 'Belladonna'.

MATERIALS FOR A DESCRIPTION OF CAPRI, 10 parts (1904–15). Parts 1,
2, 7, 9, 10, London; parts 3–6, 8, Naples.

1. The Blue Grotto and its Literature, 1904.

2. The Forestal Conditions of Capri, 1904.

3. Fabio Giordano's Relation of Capri, 1906.

4. The Lost Literature of Capri, 1906.

5. Tiberius, 1906.

6. Saracens and Corsairs in Capri, 1906.

7. The Life of the Venerable Suor Serafina di Dio, 1907.

8. Some Antiquarian Notes, 1907.

9. Disiecta Membra, 1915.

10. Index, 1915.

Republished as CAPRI: Materials for a Description of the Island,
Florence (1930).

SIREN LAND (1911; new and revised edition, 1923). *Travel.*

FOUNTAINS IN THE SAND. RAMBLES AMONG THE OASES OF TUNISIA (1912).
Travel.

OLD CALABRIA (1915). *Travel.*
A reprint of 1956 contains a valuable Introduction by J. Davenport.

LONDON STREET GAMES (1916; second edition, revised and enlarged,
1931). *Essay.*

SOUTH WIND (1917; new edition with Introduction 1946). *Fiction.*

THEY WENT (1920). *Fiction.*
The third impression, 1921, has a Prefatory Letter and contains
changes in the text.

ALONE (1921). *Travel.*

TOGETHER (1923). *Travel.*

D. H. LAWRENCE AND MAURICE MAGNUS. A plea for better manners. Privately printed, Florence (1924).
A reply to D. H. Lawrence's Introduction to *Memoirs of the Foreign Legion* by Maurice Magnus.

EXPERIMENTS (1925). *Essays and Reviews.*
Includes: 'Arabia Deserta', 'The Correct Thing', 'Blind Guides', 'At the Forge', 'Edgar Allan Poe', 'Belladonna', 'Intellectual Nomadism', 'The Last Word', 'A Mad Englishman', 'Queer', 'Anacreonic'.

IN THE BEGINNING (1928). *Fiction.*
A privately printed limited edition appeared in Florence in 1927.

BIRDS AND BEASTS OF THE GREEK ANTHOLOGY (1928). *Essays.*
A privately printed edition was published in Florence in 1927.

HOW ABOUT EUROPE? Some footnotes on East and West (1929). *Commentary.*
A privately printed edition appeared in Florence in 1928.
Stimulated by the production in 1927 of *Mother India* by K. Mayo.

ONE DAY, Chapelle-Réanville (1929). *Travel.*
Included in *Three of Them*, 1930.

THREE OF THEM (1930). *Essays.*
'One Day', 'Nerinda', 'On the Herpetology of the Grand Duchy ot Baden'.

Introduction to [THE LAST OF THE MEDICI by John Gaston de Medici, Grand Duke of Tuscany, done in the English by H. Acton. Privately printed, Florence (1930).]

PANEROS. Some words on Aphrodisiacs and the like (1931). *Essay.*
A privately printed edition appeared in Florence in 1930.

SUMMER ISLANDS. Ischia and Ponza (1931; limited edition, 1944). *Travel.*

LOOKING BACK. An Autobiographical Excursion, 2 vols. (1933). *Autobiography.* One volume edition, 1934.

LATE HARVEST (1946). *Autobiography.*

FOOTNOTE ON CAPRI (1952). *Notes with illustrations.*

VENUS IN THE KITCHEN or Love's Cookery Book by Pilaff Bey. Edited by Norman Douglas. Introduction by G. Greene (1952).
At least half of this treatise was composed by Douglas's friend and publisher, G. Orioli.

Some Biographical and Critical Studies:

NORMAN DOUGLAS, by H. M. Tomlinson (1931).
Reprinted with additions, 1952.

NORMAN DOUGLAS, by R. MacGillivray, Florence (1933).
Re-issued London, 1952, under the author's own name, R. M. Dawkins.

NORMAN DOUGLAS: A Pictorial Record by C. Fitzgibbon (1953).
Together with a brief study.

OMNES EODEM COGIMUR: Some notes written following the death of Norman Douglas, 9 February 1952, by K. Macpherson.
Privately printed 1953.

GRAND MAN, by N. Cunard (1954).

At the time of going to press the following books by Norman Douglas were in print on Messrs. Chatto and Windus's list: *Looking Back*; *An Almanac*; *Experiments*; and a Selection from his works with an Introduction by D. M. Low, which is published jointly with Messrs. Secker and Warburg.

South Wind, and *Old Calabria*, with an Introduction by John Davenport, were published by Messrs. Secker and Warburg, who have in preparation new editions of *Siren Land* and *Fountains in the Sand*.

WRITERS AND THEIR WORK

Available at 2s. net each; starred titles at 1s. 6d. net each

MATTHEW ARNOLD: Kenneth Allott
JANE AUSTEN*: Sylvia Townsend
 Warner
HILAIRE BELLOC: Renée Haynes
ARNOLD BENNETT*: Frank
 Swinnerton
WILLIAM BLAKE*: Kathleen Raine
JAMES BOSWELL: P. A. W. Collins
ELIZABETH BOWEN: Jocelyn Brooke
THE BRONTË SISTERS: P. Bentley
BUNYAN: Henri Talon
SAMUEL BUTLER: G. D. H. Cole
BYRON*: Herbert Read
THOMAS CARLYLE*: D. Gascoyne
JOYCE CARY: Walter Allen
CHAUCER: Nevill Coghill
G. K. CHESTERTON: Christopher Hollis
WINSTON CHURCHILL: John Connell
COLERIDGE: Kathleen Raine
R. G. COLLINGWOOD: E. W. F.
 Tomlin
I. COMPTON-BURNETT*: Pamela
 Hansford Johnson
JOSEPH CONRAD: Oliver Warner
GEORGE CRABBE: R. L. Brett
C. DAY LEWIS: Clifford Dyment
DEFOE: J. R. Sutherland
CHARLES DICKENS: K. J. Fielding
JOHN DRYDEN: Bonamy Dobrée
GEORGE ELIOT*: Lettice Cooper
T. S. ELIOT: M. C. Bradbrook
FIELDING: John Butt
FORD MADOX FORD: Kenneth Young
E. M. FORSTER: Rex Warner
CHRISTOPHER FRY: Derek Stanford
EDWARD GIBBON: C. V. Wedgwood
ROBERT GRAVES: M. Seymour-Smith
GRAHAM GREENE: Francis Wyndham
JOHN GALSWORTHY: R. H. Mottram
THOMAS HARDY*: R. A. Scott-James
G. M. HOPKINS: Geoffrey Grigson
A. E. HOUSMAN: Ian Scott-Kilvert
ALDOUS HUXLEY: Jocelyn Brooke
HENRY JAMES: Michael Swan

SAMUEL JOHNSON: S. C. Roberts
JOHN KEATS: Edmund Blunden
RUDYARD KIPLING*: Bonamy
 Dobrée
CHARLES LAMB: Edmund Blunden
D. H. LAWRENCE: Kenneth Young
WYNDHAM LEWIS: E. W. F. Tomlin
KATHERINE MANSFIELD: Ian A.
 Gordon
WALTER DE LA MARE: K. Hopkins
MARLOWE: Philip Henderson
JOHN MASEFIELD*: L. A. G. Strong
SOMERSET MAUGHAM*: J. Brophy
MILTON: E. M. W. Tillyard
WILLIAM MORRIS: Philip Henderson
EDWIN MUIR: J. C. Hall
JOHN HENRY NEWMAN:
 J. M. Cameron
GEORGE ORWELL: Tom Hopkinson
POPE: Ian Jack
HERBERT READ: Francis Berry
RUSKIN: Peter Quennell
BERTRAND RUSSELL*: Alan Dorward
BERNARD SHAW*: A. C. Ward
SHAKESPEARE: C. J. Sisson
SHELLEY: Stephen Spender
SHERIDAN*: W. A. Darlington
EDITH SITWELL: John Lehmann
OSBERT SITWELL*: Roger Fulford
TOBIAS SMOLLETT*: L. Brander
STERNE: D. W. Jefferson
R. L. STEVENSON: G. B. Stern
LYTTON STRACHEY: R. A.
 Scott-James
SWIFT: J. Middleton Murry
SWINBURNE: H. J. C. Grierson
G. M. TREVELYAN*: J. H. Plumb
EVELYN WAUGH: Christopher Hollis
H. G. WELLS: Montgomery Belgion
OSCAR WILDE: James Laver
CHARLES WILLIAMS: J. Heath-Stubbs
IZAAK WALTON: Margaret Bottrall
VIRGINIA WOOLF: Bernard Blackstone
WORDSWORTH: Helen Darbishire
W. B. YEATS: G. S. Fraser

The first 55 issues in the Series appeared under the
General Editorship of T. O. BEACHCROFT

¶ Essays in active preparation include assessments of Spenser, Tennyson, Rossetti,
Dylan Thomas and other classics and contemporaries.

WRITERS AND THEIR WORK

★

A NEW ISSUE in this series on Writers and their
Work is published monthly and may be ordered from
any bookseller or, in case of difficulty, direct from the
Publishers, LONGMANS, GREEN & CO. LTD., 6 &
7 Clifford Street, London W.1.

Annual subscriptions (12 issues)   22s. 6d. post free
Six months' subscription (6 issues)   12s. post free
Single issues   2s. each
(Back numbers available at 1s. 6d. and 2s. each—for
list of titles see inside cover.)

★

BRITISH BOOK NEWS, to which these essays
form supplements, is published monthly and may be
obtained from The British Council, 65 Davies Street,
London W.1. In addition to an article of general or
bibliographical interest, each issue contains short, informative and critical reviews, by specialists, of some 200
books. Every subject is covered, including fiction and
children's books, and full details of publisher, price, size,
etc., are given. Annual subscription: U.K. 24s. (or 26s.★);
U.S.A. and Canada $3.50 (or $3.70★); other countries
10s. (or 12s.★).

★ With Annual Index